Masks of the Dreamer

The Wesleyan Poetry Program : Volume 96

Masks
of the Dreamer

POEMS BY

Mike Lowery

Wesleyan University Press
MIDDLETOWN, CONNECTICUT

Grateful acknowledgement is made to the following publications, in which some of these poems have appeared: *Aura, The Cape Rock, Coe Review, Green's Magazine, Huron Review, Impact, Kansas Quarterly, Lake Superior Review, Nimrod, Pawn Review, Poetry: People, Poetry View, Quartet, South & West, Studies in Poetry, Tightrope, West End, Wind, Xanadu.*

Library of Congress Cataloging in Publication Data

Lowery, Mike, 1941–
    Masks of the dreamer.

        (Wesleyan poetry program; 96)
        I. Title.
PS3562.0896M3   811'.5'4   79-65336
ISBN 0-8195-2096-9
ISBN 0-8195-1096-3 pbk.

Manufactured in United States of America
First edition

To my son Michael

I
Roots

The Homecoming

I was born in Kansas City on September 18,
1910, and was the baby of the family. My
sister Katherine Lowery—now she's Kate Woods,
which is her married name—is three or four
years older, and she used to say my mother
spoiled me. My mother made her take me
wherever she went. My father was a brakeman
on the Frisco Railroad, and he was a
fisherman too. He caught catfish down
in the river bottom. But I don't know
much about him. He was killed by a
train when I was three or four, and I was
raised by my mama and my grandmother.

Early last June I moved back to the white
frame house where I spent my childhood.
After all those years the house was huddled
and rain-streaked, with the doleful face of
my aunt Edna haunting the kitchen window.

I wander from room to room checking objects
against my memory.

I think not of the summers past but of all
summers. Of sitting on the front porch under
a crowded night sky. And yet, I can remember
the contents of a dresser drawer—green glass
marbles, a brown fountain pen, a pair of broken
sunglasses and a deck of Bicycle playing cards
as stiff as my knee.

Small Desolations

it's strange
after all these years
I still half-remember
a walled strip of school gravel
the bleached portico of a Romanesque building
a wooden desk
steaming radiators
and the musty odor of damp coats

when I was nine years old
Mrs. Grant
my third-grade teacher
showed the class
color slides of her trip to Italy
in Pompeii there was a small dog
wide-eyed with terror
still chained to its post

these small desolations
bind me to the past

Deep Water

when I was a boy
I used to find myself
on the last day of summer vacation
seeing for the first time
the outline of trees against the sky
and the magic light and color
of the water I had been
swimming in for weeks

Today
hidden from yellow lakes of sunlight
I find myself in the deep
shade of tall buildings
where I float among
mortgages
credit cards
and charge accounts

surrounded by typists with heavy legs
who wear clothes that try too hard

Family Portrait

My father has lived in a three-bedroom
frame house on the west side of the city
for more than twenty years. It's a middle-
class neighborhood that was once white
working-class and is now black—"colored"
as he usually says.

He's been retired for years. What does
he do with his days and nights? He putters.
He tinkers. He walks to supermarket and
back. He cooks his meals. He watches T.V.

His home is dusty. At the end of the hall
I smell an odor, dry and ancient. It is
the totem of old families.

The Glass Path

Aunt Edna's dining room was filled with
Nordic Blue plates, imported from the old
country. They were wired to the walls.
They policed me.

One afternoon she saw something she called
inconvenient going on in the woodshed.

Aunt Edna and her plates are lost in
remembrance, colored by time and
distorted by memory. But I still see
clearly her squinty eyes behind dowdy
glasses, her plump body inside a frumpy,
printed housedress as she warned me
against the path taken by some family
black sheep.

Years later I learned her own tortured
path led her down a ramshackle hallway
of broken glass.

Moving from
Red Fork, Oklahoma, 1956

the past fell into the
sea, we moved downtown and
cast our vote to live like
rich-folk, in dream houses from
FHA. and found cellars of a sunless
earth, and blue electric dawn.

Matinee

I grew up
in Saturday afternoon darkness
embossed
by silver screens

now
I spend stale beer afternoons
in a city of glass walls
among hum-colored cars
where
I hide for no reason

and think
of days
when I could smell the rain

Brother

1.

the frost chain
broke, iron nails in
a drifting log made
the world dark.

2.

my voice, soft as
water echoed your
name to a thin
colorless face.

3.

mama said don't be
afraid, touch him; at
night water washes my arm
like a dead tree on a dark pond.

4.

the birds are far away. no
longer does the oak begin
the wind and leaves brush open
stars. or birds fly
through the ring in the moon.

The Wild Blue Yonder

in Hopkins' five & dime
I bought model airplanes
trading coins for
dreams. I, the shy
underfed mama's
boy who was going to fly
someday.

Sister

you said red hair made you
different, in the
alchemy of memory I still
see two clock lost
wanderers fumbling for
lucky strikes behind
Whitner's dry goods store.
losing track of time in our
search for magicians and poets

I danced in iron
shoes– ah but
you, on the edge of
the fire pit, lit by
the flames of the jukebox, danced
in the wild heart of the fire.

till, with a baby in
your belly, you became
a fearful bird, ever
hearing the hawk's bell.

The House Was Always Dark
after Father Died

I always helped after school. I dusted the
china, fed the canary, swept the livingroom
floor, and always wiped my shoes before
letting in the sun.

Mother and I were always together. In the
evening we watched the bible-black night
through painted window panes. The light touch
of cobwebs held us together for twenty-seven
years.

Today we meet under a glass bell; we sing
hymns on Sunday afternoons, while Thorazine
melts the sky.

I I
The World

The Marketplace

it is a street of
butchers
clockmakers
tailors
and bakers
toothless old women
shopkeepers
nearly senile
in partnership with white-haired men

I buy meat
watch every slice of the knife
and every knot of lard

an old woman talks of
a dance hall long ago
still shy
still courting
the baker dreams of dough not rising

The Visit

In a city of corporations and glassed-in
dreams an old woman sits in front of a
rain-streaked window. We talk. I try to
imagine that I belonged to those times.
They are dead and they are not dead.

From beneath her flower-trimmed straw hat she
reminds me of deck chairs and languid
afternoons of cricket. Nervously fingering
her seed-pearl necklace she speaks of her
grandson, who wears steel-rimmed Russian-
revolutionary glasses and reads *Ho Chi
Minh: A Political Biography*.

But, in the summer of 1926 her body's
splendor brought Greece to Kansas and
Kalamazoo. Her spirit was green as a
bay tree. Her flesh was not yet worn by
the weight of laurels. On Sunday afternoons
her Greek dance flourished in the Catskills,
where under the summer spruce metaphysics
and muscles were welded.

No longer does her body speak in heroic
sculptural movements. She listens only to
the ancient concerns of her body's crude
claims. And sits inert, a battered pagan
tomb along the Sacred Way between Eleusis
and the city of the Parthenon.

Wine and Water

I pull my hat over my eyes and turn my coat
collar against the wind. Down the stairs I
run toward the river, past the D.A.R. graveyard.

At the foot of the stairs an old sailor lies ship-
wrecked under a tree, sleeping, drinking and dreaming
of ancient women who open their legs to the sun.
He no longer follows streets. He now seeks only rivers.
He has become a tramp steamer sailing over
mysterious river bottoms where iron chains of
loneliness anchor discarded barges at the edge of
the water.

I grew up thinking the river was a woman. Now,
women feed the river. I become a sea creature,
boneless beneath the jellyfish bell of my own coat.

The Children's Hour

In the maze of my old neighborhood I leaf
through my scrapbook. A spell is cast
from page to page. I become yellowed
among the pages of childhood.

On the corner, at the end of the block,
stands an old clapboard two-story
white house.

During the bored hours of the lodging-
house day I share the drooping domestic
lives of the local whores. I wait for
early evening darkness to turn the white
boards blue.

In the curdled darkness I become a
haunted man playing children's games.
I follow girls with hollow eyes up
dark stairs.

The Incident

at night I dump cats
by the side of the road
where toads fold into
stone. by day I build
crosses of Bethlehem
steel. and cry at
the death of strangers.

after work I drink
beer at the Country Gentlemen
bar. plot crimes of
passion and omission till
the bar maid mothers me home.

haunted by dream
fathers, my bullet baptizes
you in the water of
the moon. I hear the dog
howl in your chest.

Crazy Alice

yesterday
crazy Alice gave me a painting
today
she whistles for her cat
he does not hear her

on my wall
a red thallophyte
swims into the protozoan
paint of her blue world
where yellow shark
teeth become framed
in an ear bone of whale

while inside her
stone house
the Katzenjammer kids
dance at dawn
as she tosses quarters
to the organ grinder

Winter Grass

with the mind of a mathematician
and the doubt of a scholar
I still see Angelica
her long hair plaited
somehow always barefoot
and in the middle of a fresh mowed lawn

when we were seven
we spent rainy afternoons
hiding in closets
full of musty grown-up clothes
while yellow muslin curtains
hid the sunlit world outside

now I look through
gray newsreel curtains
onto a decaying garden
and phony flickering gaslights

gaunt and sad-eyed
I try to put things in order
salt air enters my dreams
cutting the long grass of winter

Cesarean

Saturday night
Strikeaxe Oklahoma
friends fetch Doc Boon from
the back room of Ruby's bar

I scrub the table

I move like a blind horse
draw water from the well
boil it on a black stove belly

a knife cuts
the root hold of earth

Raisin' Anchor

my hotwaterbottled body's been
that blind sailor's bus stop too long
I'm packin' up my candlewick calico
and bedsocks and driftin' down
those sea dark streets

now he can belly over in bedclothes
with all the bare bold girls in the world

Kate's Place

Kate was raised on a Nebraska farm, with her sisters
and brother. Their father used to say, "If you don't
work, you don't eat."

When Kate first reached Chicago, she scratched at
the sidewalk to see if grass would grow; then she
tried to get a job. She started in the Stockyards
for thirty-seven cents an hour. She lied, and told
the bosses she had experience in butchering on the
farm back home. She was seventeen.

To keep your job, she learned, you don't talk, you
just do your work.

Forty years later, she still don't talk much. She
lives alone in a two-room walk-up near the Loop.
Her room is used, the way she is used.

Summary Dance

1.

Having neither money nor virtue I spend
long afternoons in the park watching
upside-down trees float on ice-green
water.

I dream of old naked days spent on
flesh pillows when I was a moth lost
in the brilliance of chandeliers.

The costume ball is over. My money
has long since disappeared into the
mouths of horses and the stockings of
ballet girls.

It's Sunday, the bells ring for no
reason.

2.

It was in the summer of '69 when I
first met Isadora. She earned her
name from her mother because her
father cruised dance halls on New
York's Lower East Side. Her father
danced out of her life when she was
three months old.

Her face was long and thin, powdered
dead white. She had green eyes that
were charcoaled with mascara.

We met under a jade goblet sky held by
dirty hands. I gripped tight her late
blooming flower, till covered by the

fugue of night we found ourselves in
a secret cafe that stood on the outskirts
of Hot Springs. I wore a beard. It's
painful to be born again, so idle and
drunken I wandered among tables drowning
my faith wine.

I followed her white angel hips down
a dark hallway. A Tiffany lamp spread
its wings in the dark room at the end
of the hall.

Opening like a marigold her rhythm
drained my secrets.

3.

In the thin milk of morning I saw
her hair straggled from a knot on top
of her head. She became an old-faced
doll with worn slippers and a robe
pinned together with two safety pins.

We celebrated the feast of fallen angels.

Bonnie Beach, 8th Grade Cheerleader

I stand in your shadow as
you squeeze into
a size fourteen dress.

my life becomes a series
of music lessons,
tap-dancing and pep clubs.

at night you sleep on the sofa
and ask yourself why the
1959 Porter peach festival queen
gave up her crown for love?

Susan Sparrow
1963 Graduate
Bryan Business School

restless fingers caress my
cast iron lover; while
meek knees tremble.

electric machine gun
swings across fluorescent
dawn, searching out
white-collar guerrillas.

the advance continues.

The Hours between Dog & Wolf

It is the Epiphany, the feast of the Three
Kings. In Spain it is the festival of the
children.

I search for exhaustion in an Elysian
whorehouse. Outside the streets are
stitched with white wool. The snow-covered
Coney Island buildings loom like Spanish
galleons.

In a small room at the end of a narrow
street I chain smoke cigarettes and wait
for night to fall. It's all the rooms I've
ever slept in, above all the streets I've
ever walked.

III
The City

The City Came Fat with
an Apple in Its Mouth

I first saw you
beneath golden arches
smoking Virginia Slims
and wearing a jade
necklace made from
the green tiles
of pigeon wings

you remind me
of small rooms where
people wave
before they jump
from windows
as you sit
well-dressed
with careful make-up
waiting to be pulled down

Tree House

deep
in the forest of the city
rain makes mud
grow on sidewalks
as I drive through
the neon night
to my burglar-proof high-rise

where
I am fed by television

till
morning drives down
from the mountain
cementing me to the city

Nite Lite

I barter myself by the hour
frozen inside a fluorescent cube
which at five o'clock drops
into a car pool and floats
me through a subterranean
city of stifling houses
and staggering churches
of a backwater town

afternoon drifts into evening
my world becomes flooded with
billboards
burger-joints
and cheap motels

anchored in the endless day of a neon lobby
I mock the night outside

The Late Show

I live alone in a furnished room,
without a car, retired because any
two-bit chiseler can shove me around.
I'm old and sick with a perforated
ulcer. I can't take being roughed-up
anymore.

Every night just before closing I go
to the Crown Drug Store. Old man
Dooley's son Jim works the counter.
He has a face like a ripe peach. His
hair is fair and thick, and grows low
on his forehead. He calls me Pop
and gives me handouts. I sweep up and
then go home.

I've never met the woman who lives
upstairs. The boys at Arnie's Bar call
her night-train Sally. In the dark I
lie on a daybed and hear her move
through the night in sweaty satin; she's
all curves and come-ons. She could make
me do anything.

I move inside a nightmare I've known for
a long time.

A Ghost Torn by the Sun

sweaty yard hands hoist
sisal sinews
as late afternoon awnings
hide the sun

haunted by the ghost of a ruined gambler
I carry my guilt from old monasteries
to dark bars
where I dice for drinks

after cutting the thin blue rope of smoke
I become a jester in the shadows
while indifferent whores
and priests slake my thirst

in a world
where legless beggars drink at dawn
I drink the watered silk of night

Welfare Refuge

I stand in the rain smoking
damp cigarettes
my world unfolds
beneath a naked sixty-watt bulb

flowered curtains
thin and frayed
blind rain-streaked windows

sometimes at night I think
the doorbell rings
once I got up and answered it
nobody was there

my sister says if her baby lives
the welfare will give her a place
with two bedrooms
if it dies
she has to stay put

Map

dawn is a long way off
I listen to country-and-western
music on the radio

it's morning
a bottle of Henry McKenna's whiskey
sits empty on the kitchen cabinet
while I cut bacon with rusty scissors

the man from the finance company
came again today
he wanted to know when I'm going to pay
he says I only have ten days left

old paint blisters
into the map of my life

Leaves of Loneliness

the city ferments
I daydream in traffic
past strips of stores and shopping malls
which sprout leaves of asphalt parking lots

I lobotomize the afternoon
at the Woodland Lounge
with an unwanted older woman

smiles and frowns pass over us
words branch out
then fall to earth

through leaves of loneliness
we roll like car-struck dogs

Sally's World

from a rented room without curtains
my iron nail words
drive into Sally's oak plank world

a world
harsh and boned down
by my macho leather
and raw mythic urges

drawn together
inside a sawdust freak show
we move in the hard-edged light of
laundromats
supermarkets
and all-night diners
dressed in each other's shadow

On the Edge of the Fat White City

on the edge of the fat white city
my red station wagon anchors
a house of stone blocks

on Sunday afternoon
the steel blade of my lawn mower
laughs at the pale grass and
memories of old summers

when you stood naked
and simple above the bed
your body an alphabet
written by the softening
chalk of my bones

now
children drink me in through
windows ten years thick
stacking my days like
alphabet blocks
one upon the other

IV
The Road

Sundowning

old was somebody else
on the cover of the *Saturday
Evening Post*
till I found myself
sitting in a morris chair
watching mountains chase
the sun
at night I turn
to face the dragon and
relive eighty-six years

a cinder finds my eye
I sit on father's lap
it is my first trip to
Hot Springs where
mother takes the waters
the train pulls out of
Red Fork and rumbles
toward the sea
past the rubble of years

I wake with secrets
buried below tidemark

Changes

I spend bright
days on Arkansas
river sand bars
watching white-bellied
birds follow wave
licks while they
search for fish

the roots of lavender thistles
fight sand and
wait for spring floods

the rains come
I stumble over the
stubble of years
my hands make shadow birds
on the wall

girls bloom out of reach

Chrome Green Memories

the leaves have come out
streams have warmed
young girls who work in mid-town offices
sun themselves on their lunch hour

yesterday
I hid souvenirs and prophecies
behind rows of slant-topped desks
today
all I remember is George Washington
in Stuart's unfinished version
forever staring through tall windows
onto the skeletal village
of swing sets and jungle gyms
while my world fills with relics of
books
chalk
crayons
and snub-nosed scissors

I think of these things as I sit alone
on a chrome green bench in Bennet Park

the sun becomes a bright weapon
boning me like the sharp knife of silence

Time Bomb

it's the last cold day of winter
the bar fills with smoke

my body fights the numbness
that creeps
past the watch on my arm

my mainspring breaks
I fall through time

dimly reflected in the mirror
I see a small boy
squinting into the sun
one hand steadies his bike
streamers hang from the handlebars
he wears a cowboy vest over
a plain shirt and jeans
a toy gunbelt hangs from one hip

the reflection of late afternoon
slides into evening

I become a moth
batting against the glass

Recollections of Aunt Edna

I spend most of my days right here in this chair
I use the footstool more now
since I've been havin' so much trouble
with my feet
I have a hard time gettin' around
even with this cane

papa was a farmer
I chopped and picked cotton
as a girl in east Texas
I was married when I was fifteen
I first met Jake
my husband
at a Methodist church party
I remember we played a game
called "Going to Jerusalem"
in the game there weren't as
many chairs as there were players
the person left standing
was "it" for the next round

we had two sons and a daughter
I cared for the kids
the house
and the garden
did the canning and sewing
and helped with the cotton chopping and picking
when the crops needed it

here in the nursing home
no one seems to care that I know how
to keep meat in salt water
and can vegetables in brine or vinegar

I don't get to cook here either
but I sure would like some
beans with hot peppers
wilted lettuce
bell peppers stuffed with cabbage
poke salad
or corn bread

the doctor keeps me on a salt-free diet
so all I've got now is television

The Long Road

I am getting old
I am getting fat

a broken arm follows me
through a quiet courtyard

my childhood has been
swallowed up by school

I lug up the mountain
in second gear behind the
wheel of a broken-down Dodge

Sea of Memory

my thoughts carry me quietly
like a gondola
through a long street of red brick
so faded that it looks silver-gray

I drift among slated roofs
back to the Bridgewater nursing home
where I float in a sea of memory

suddenly
it's the summer of 1910
on Brighton beach
I've misplaced my straw hat
the Panama with the wide brim
the wind begins to make swirls of sand
rain down on my knees
I notice the pearl-gray sky
above a black sea

then
my mind becomes confused
my jaw grows slack
I listen for the sea moan
in my old belly

The Harvest

I have climbed peach trees
sailed sticks on rain ponds
wandered past
starched shirtfront faces
which hid the dark
frailty of shopkeepers
and smelled the smell
of everyday life
beneath small town rain

now
clock-watching
I follow time
nothing but time

as peaches slowly ripen

Retirement

I begin again
I do not move forward

my family makes excuses for my
failing memory and trembling hands

unexpected
without fanfare
I stand in silence before them

unable to hear their whispers
I pretend not to see them

I am retired
but I am busy with them

V
The Myths

The Blood Flowers of Mary Long-Legs

I set out into the forest. I do not fear
to be alone. There is in my bearing the
magnificence of a barbarian who tramples
flowers beneath his boots.

From the forest I merge with gangsters,
burglars and pimps. I journey across a
bleak landscape full of all-night diners,
cheap hotels, truckstops, pool halls,
strip joints, Greyhound buses, double
knits, jumper cables, Naugahyde
luncheonette booths, hashbrowns, six-
packs and C.B. radios.

Yesterday I saw God– he lives in a flop-
house– he was sitting on the steps of
Orpha's Bar & Grill, he needed a shave.

I search for Mary Long-Legs. My
pilgrimage takes me to the side of a wild
mountain where a grotto was hewn in heathen
times. The grotto is circular, wide, high
and with upright walls, snow-white, smooth
and plain. Above, the vault is finely
joined, and on the keystone there is a
flower, embellished with jewels. The floor
is smooth rich marble, green as grass. In
the center stands a bed.

On the bed my Angel of the Apocalypse lies
tangled in damp and rumpled sheets. She
appears as white and sunken as an avalanche,
her heavy eyelids hide pagan eyes which
reflect my face which has become the
desperate face of a mystic.

I am intimidated by her, for she is beautiful
and she is mad.

I am her tomb. The earth is nothing. I
search for the stigmata on her thigh.

A snake is kept in a golden chest and at
the hour of the mysteries loaves are heaped
upon the table to summon the serpent.

Mary Long-Legs becomes a Vegas blackjack
dealer and walks with her hips stuck out
in a slow insinuation as drawling as her
talk.

My lips kiss prayers from a pair of broken
bones.

The front door stands ajar. Inside a
smokey dive One-Eyed Jack is playing
Leadbelly blues. The serpentine music
unrolls in the dark shadows, curling
round the wrists and necks of whores who
happen to be walking past, their milky
thighs slithering under clinging black satin.

With my primitive cock and mind I dance the
smoke and smoke the music.

In a black Edwardian dress Mary arches her
back as we dance a fox-trot inside a doll
house. We dance around the dirge where
last night we died three times.

The fox-trot changes to a tango. We are
locked up in a monument of murmurs. Bright

as a slaughterhouse knife I cleave her. We
noiselessly come together.

Mary Long-Legs is trapped in a sumptuous mid-
town apartment which is adorned with gold,
its walls are hung with garnet-red velvet.
On the ceiling are large beveled mirrors.
There is no furniture, only thick green
carpets.

I keep her away from sun, stars and dreams.
She is nourished by her own sun, her own
stars, and her own dreams. I move slowly
around her. I do not touch her.

Despite her being cloistered, despite her
soft captivity, her nobility rests grail-
like between her legs.

Lost trains run over Babylonian rooftops.
Sirens with their lodestone call me.

I continue my journey to the Holy Land; my
head is full of roads, roads to Byzantium,
roads to the ramparts of Jerusalem.

A slave of my baptism I dream of crusades
and unrecorded voyages. At the end of the
street I see a huge stone angel.

Our Age of Fable

I.

I am alone in a noble room, a room
hung with strips of shining silk.
The curtains hang on red-gold rings,
and have a rope pull. Silk tapestries
cover the walls.

I am a knight errant with a fleur-de-
lis on my shoulder. I wear a worsted
suit, scented linen, a chain on my
wrist, and a tie as fluid as a
tongue of flame and shoes—black
patent, narrow and pointed.

Surrounded by the dens of witches,
I chant the hours in an underground
thronged with bouncers, queers and
whores. God enters my soul like a
gigolo who cruises a tea room.
Magic wafer words thicken the
darkness within the great hall.

Outside the wild wind runs to
wrestle with the sun till the
Michaelmas moon promises snow.

I play dice and knuckle bones in
the dark while cat-footed guards
wait for night to end.

Thus, I begin my quest for rare
sights and autistic visions.

2.

My lady's wild eyes are full of
cocaine and flowers. Her heart
beats quick with the music, she
calls me her snake fisher of the
wedding feast, prisoner of sheets
lost in the matted wilderness of
her hair. Her Eve-hipped ancient
meanings and slow rites take me
down through the botany of the
underworld where I join princes,
astrologers and pornographers in
the search for the Holy Grail.

3.

Dogs run free, and the forest swells
with horns, hooves and chases.

Inside, thousands of white candles
hanging in rings of gold and crystal
melt onto green marble floors. The
waxed torches kindle a clear bright
light on my face, a face gentle and
violent. I was born to be a pimp.

When I was a kid in Saint Louis, the
girls were called babes. But when
you found out a girl could be had,
she became a bimbo.

4.

In my war against winter I wear over
my doublet of Tharsia silk a hood,
tied at the neck and lined with thick
fur. My white silk shirt is embroidered

with parrots perched among painted
purple flowers, and turtledoves, and
lover's knots so thick that ladies
could have sewn them for seven winters.

I spend long evenings mulling my wine.
I try my flesh with simple food while
holy women drink my name before a
long table laid on a trestle.

In a rain of ashes I wait for the
powder keg of morning. A secret door
opens on a dark but elegant stairway.
I hear masses being said at the end
of the hall where Saints drink sherry
and smoke Havana cigars. Beneath
this night shade of nicotine I give
my heart to the King, my cock to the
whores, my head to the hangman.
And then dance and mime with subtle
magic through this enchanted night,
canonized in the warm belly of a
frail sisterhood.

5.

As winter nears its end I prepare to
leave the castle of the sinner King.
Each year I set forth without shield
when the flat earth opens into flowers
and fields and plains grow thick and
green. By the faith of my body I
seek marvels no tongue can tell. I
become a ghost torn by the sun, no
longer a pale child prisoner. I
ride where men go astray.

Joan of the Rusty Rose

I measure change from my purse
of flesh, spending it on seasons of
large and little deaths.

It is the evening before my execution. I
wear the white robe of the doomed. I stain
the calendar page. In the darkness of
my cell I wash myself in the bucket
from which I drink.

With blood I write scared signs
on the darkness, signs of the cross
that merge with pentacles.

I drink blood and wine.
I listen to the witches of Lorraine.

Siege Perilous

the old year is dying

I seek the Grail with my sword
and move in a casual course
from one adventure to the next
trusting women more than God
each evening I journey forth
into a forest of garish colored lights
amplified disco music
and busty bespangled maidens
wrapped in spun-sugar candy

my lust carries me to an elegant
long-legged girl with shiny
bright-red lipstick
and hair pulled up into dime-store combs
she wears
high-heeled shoes
cigarette-leg pants made of Reynolds wrap
and a gauzy
gold-embroidered lilac kurta

we dance
with our hands on each other's hips

I burn my thoughts with the old year
along with my bundle of lost chances